YOU GO, GIRL

You Go, Girl: How Women Build Up the Church

Published by Know The Truth
P.O. Box 30250
Anaheim, CA 92809-0208
(888) 644-8811

Scripture quotations are from the ESV® Bible (The Holy Bible, English Standard Version®), copyright © 2001 by Crossway, a publishing ministry of Good News Publishers. Used by permission. All rights reserved.

ISBN 978-1-7360801-1-5

Cover art design by Fluid Communications, Inc.

Copyright © 2021 by Know The Truth
Layout design provided by Fluid Communications, Inc.
Italics in Scripture quotations reflect the author's added emphasis.
All rights reserved. No part of this book may be reproduced
or transmitted in any form or by any means, electronic or mechanical,
including photocopying and recording, or by any information storage
and retrieval system, without permission in writing from the publisher.
The only exception is brief quotations in printed reviews.

Published in the United States by Know The Truth, Anaheim, California.

YOU GO, GIRL

HOW WOMEN BUILD UP THE CHURCH

PHILIP DE COURCY

Contents

INTRODUCTION i

CHAPTER 1:
THE PURPOSE OF WOMEN IN THE BIBLE 1

CHAPTER 2:
THE PROMINENCE OF WOMEN IN THE BIBLE 9

CHAPTER 3:
THE PARTICIPATION OF WOMEN IN THE BIBLE 19

ACKNOWLEDGEMENTS 35

ENDNOTES 37

Introduction

In his excellent book *The Unquenchable Flame: Discovering the Heart of the Reformation*, Michael Reeves tells an unusual but fascinating story about a great English Protestant archbishop by the name of Thomas Cranmer.[1]

Prior to being appointed as the Archbishop of Canterbury, Cranmer was a priest and spent some time in Lutheran Germany. While he was there, he did something that priests were forbidden from doing in England—he fell in love with a girl and married her. It was a risky move, particularly as he was suddenly and unexpectedly elevated to the position of archbishop. What would he do about this secret marriage? Because the stakes were so high, he decided that for a time it would be best to hide his bride, Margarete. So, Thomas constructed a box. Everywhere they went, Margarete went into the box. Thomas did drill a few holes into the side of the box so that she could breathe—he did love her after all. But wherever Thomas went, his dear wife rode with him in the box. Church historians have called Margarete Cranmer one of the minor martyrs of the Protestant Reformation for enduring the inconvenience of jumping in and out of the box every time her husband traveled somewhere—not to mention all of those times the box was packed upside-down! Can you imagine him at Customs? They would ask, "Do you have anything to declare?"

This story of Mrs. Cranmer in a box is strange, but it is also a powerful metaphor for how women at times have been treated in the church. More often than we would like to admit, women in the church are confined to a manmade box that inhibits their ability to exercise spiritual gifts and fulfill their calling in Christ. Sometimes this happens inadvertently as we do the necessary work of commending and defending God's design for men and women. The biblical doctrine of complementarianism teaches that men and women are equal in value as image bearers of God (Gen. 1:26–27; Gal. 3:28). However, God has given men and women distinct but complementary roles, particularly in the home (Gen. 2:18; Eph. 5:22–33; 1 Pet. 3:1–7) and in the church (1 Cor. 11:2–16; 1 Tim. 2:8–3:7; Titus 1:5–9; 2:1–8). In the process of upholding this important doctrine, we can at times overemphasize what the Bible prohibits women from doing in the home, the church, and society. My concern is that beating the drum too loudly for what women *cannot* do sends the wrong message—or an incomplete message at best.

Too often we pay only lip service to the complementarian belief in the inherent equality of men and women while we emphasize the differences between the sexes. I fear this may obscure the Bible's teaching on the priesthood of *all* believers (1 Pet. 2:9; Rev. 1:5b–6). By the same token, in an earnest effort to promote the importance of Christian marriage and motherhood, we forget to remind women of the joys and privileges of singleness and God's distinct calling for women beyond the home.

So, the church, however well-intentioned, has tended in more ways than one to put women in boxes. Women are ministers to Christ and saints set apart for works of service just as men are, but we have failed to talk up and set forth the breadth and beauty of what they *can* and *must* do for the good of the church. That is why Tony Merida is right on the money when he says, "Women are to be active participants in the mission of the church. We shouldn't relegate women to the kitchen and to kids. The Great Commission is not just given to men, and spiritual gifts were not just given to men. They're given to all Christians, and women should never be sidelined in the church."[2] This is what I want you to take away from this book—that women are not inferior to men. Wives are not merely adjunct to their husbands. Women are not under house arrest and they certainly are not the B-team in the church. I want to help you see and celebrate the glorious contribution women have made to the life of the church, both in the Bible and throughout history.

Women, you have a legacy of faithful and fruitful service to the Lord to carry on. William Booth, founder of the Salvation Army, was onto something when he said, "Some of my best men are women!" They have made a vital contribution to the church and the spread of the gospel that we need to recognize. To that end, in this book we will study the purpose, the prominence, and the participation of women in the Bible as a model for you. My prayer is that it will challenge you as a woman to think outside the box and consider what God has yet to do in and through your life. I believe I am qualified to address you on two fronts. First, the Lord has called me to be a pastor and Bible teacher, and by His grace I have been ministering the Word of God to His people for more than 30 years. Second, by virtue of having a wife and three daughters, I have lived in a female dormitory for most of my life.

Some time ago I read a book called *50 Women Every Christian Should Know* by Michelle DeRusha. One of those women is named Elizabeth Fry, and she was known for bringing prison reform to Britain. As DeRusha tells of Elizabeth Fry's valuable contribution to society, she observes, "No person will deny the importance attached to the character and conduct of a woman in all her domestic and social relations, when she is filling the station of a daughter, sister, a wife, a mother or a mistress of a family.... But it is a dangerous error to suppose that the duties of females end here."[3] And it is a dangerous error—one that I want to help us think through together.

By way of clarification, the ministry of women through marriage and motherhood will not be the focus of this book. To be sure, the roles of marriage and motherhood are of utmost importance in God's design and purpose for women. They are critical to the thriving of the family, the church, and society (Titus 2:3–5). One wife and mother defined the high calling of motherhood well when asked what she did for a living: "I am socializing two homo-sapiens in the dominant values of the Judeo-Christian tradition that they may be instruments for the transformation of the social order."[4] However, we will look beyond the scope of marriage and motherhood because I want to broaden your horizon as women. I want to teach and remind you that you are something *more* than a wife and mother, if that describes you (although, again, that in itself is a vital and glorious calling in a woman's life). I want to challenge you to explore all that God has created you to do in the church and beyond.

I've always appreciated Martin Luther, the Protestant reformer. But it seems to me that he at times erred greatly. In a book about Luther and the Protestant Reformation, I came across something disconcerting he once said: "Women are created for no other purpose than to serve men and be their helpers." He also said, "If women grow weary or even die while bearing children, that doesn't harm anything. Let them bear children to death; they are created for that."[5] With all due respect, Luther has gone too far here. Women are more than servants of their husbands and baby factories. In addition to being wives and mothers, they are created in Christ Jesus unto an array of good works that God has prepared for them (Eph. 2:10).

As you know, I have entitled this book *You Go, Girl: How Women Build Up the Church*. This is my endeavor to highlight, from the Scriptures, the important contribution women have made in the church. It goes without saying that the church was established by godly men. The apostles laid the foundations of the church and then passed the torch to elders and pastors, whom they appointed in every town to lead the local congregations (Acts 15:1–35; Eph. 2:20; Titus 1:5–9). However, to overlook the role women played in the church would be a missed opportunity for learning and application. So, for the purposes of our study, we are going to examine how women have been used by God in building up His church. We will examine what Scripture says about the *purpose* for which God created women, the *prominence* of women in the Old and New Testaments, and the *participation* of women in the church. I hope our study will leave you with this message ringing in your ear: *You go, girl*—for the glory of God and His kingdom.

CHAPTER 1

The Purpose
OF WOMEN IN THE BIBLE

Let's begin at the beginning. From the opening chapters of Genesis, the inherent value of women is firmly established. Genesis 1 details God's creation of the heavens and the earth and every living creature. In Genesis 2, we zoom in for a closer look at the beginnings of man—made in the image of God and the crown jewel of His creation. God forms man from the dust of the earth and breathes the divine breath of life into him, and Adam is born (Gen. 2:7). However, as soon as He creates Adam, He notices a problem and provides a solution: "It is not good that the man should be alone; I will make him a helper fit for him" (Gen. 2:18).

A GRACIOUS SOLUTION

The Creator defines the purpose, value, and contribution of women from the outset. He presents woman as the solution to a "not good" situation. This is the first problem we find in creation. If we trace the language of Genesis 1 and 2, as God creates all living creatures in the earth, sky, and sea, we read this statement: "And God saw that it was good" (Gen. 1:21, 25). Then He makes Adam, and all of a sudden we come up short—it is *not good* that man should be alone.

In fact, the Hebrew phrase for "not good" is quite strong; it's not just *not good*—this is *bad*. We have got to fix this. The woman is God's gracious means of solving Adam's predicament. And so, God creates woman from the bone and flesh of the man (Gen. 2:21–23). Her worth and contribution are described in Genesis 2:18 in these words: "a helper comparable to him" (NKJV). Implied here is the fact that women and men are equivalent; they have the same intrinsic value as human beings and image bearers of God. She is not inferior—she is comparable to him. Although the woman is equal to the man in essence, her role and function are different from his. God gave woman the distinct purpose of being a helper to man, and He thoughtfully crafted her for this purpose. Eve was to partner with Adam in fulfilling the creation mandate: "Be fruitful and multiply and fill the earth and subdue it, and have dominion over the fish of the sea and over the birds of the heavens and over every living thing that moves on the earth" (Gen. 1:28).

Ladies, here is something I do not want you to miss, and it is a beautiful thing. In Genesis 2:18, the woman is not made the helper because she is second-rate or lacking in any way. In fact, the reason she was created was because man was lacking. Bible teacher John MacArthur highlights this important point: "The words of this verse emphasize man's need for a companion, a helper, and an equal. He was incomplete without someone to complement him in fulfilling the task of filling, multiplying, and taking dominion over the earth. This points to Adam's inadequacy, not Eve's insufficiency. Woman was made by God to meet man's deficiency."[1] Adam could not fulfill the creation mandate alone. Eve was created to make up what was lacking in Adam.

You may have heard the old story of the little girl who said at Sunday school, "God made man first, took one look at him, and said, 'I can do better.' And then He made woman." Now, that's not true, not really. But

God did make the woman upon making the man to complement him. It was only together as partners that they could complete the task God had set before humanity.

AN INDISPENSABLE HELPER

It is important to correct any misunderstanding of the term "helper." When you hear the word "helper," you might think of the movie *The Help*, which is about the experiences of two black maids in the 1960s. You might conclude that Eve was created to be Adam's domestic help—all he has to do is whistle when he wants a soda from the fridge. I want to dispel this notion immediately and completely. Woman was not made to be man's personal assistant or housekeeper. She is man's esteemed counterpart in fulfilling the joint endeavor of Genesis 1:28. Her contributions in childbearing and in the multitude of skills and gifts she brings to the relationship make her an indispensable helper to man.

The Hebrew word for "help" in Genesis 2:18, which is *ezer*, is used 21 times in the Old Testament. In 16 of those instances, it is used in reference to God Himself. He comes to Israel's rescue time and time again. They call on God for help, and He graciously assists, delivers, and saves. Listen to these descriptions of God as *ezer*:

- "There is none like God, O Jeshurun, who rides through the heavens to your *help*, through the skies in his majesty." (Deut. 33:26)
- "Our soul waits for the Lord; he is our *help* and our shield." (Ps. 33:20)
- "But I am poor and needy; hasten to me, O God! You are my *help* and my deliverer; O Lord, do not delay!" (Ps. 70:5)

The fact that *ezer* is used of Almighty God imbues this supportive role with dignity and strength. He humbly condescends to come to the aid of His people, for their good. Christ our Savior demonstrated the same humility when He came to help sinful man, in submission to His Father. Paul explains that Christ, "though he was in the form of God, did not count equality with God a thing to be grasped, but emptied himself, by taking the form of a servant, being born in the likeness of men. And being found in human form, he humbled himself by becoming obedient to the point of death, even death on a cross" (Phil. 2:6–8). Christ willingly became a servant to save sinners and accomplish God's plan of redemption. In doing so, He made helping a noble, sacred work that is pleasing to God. It is an honor for the woman to bear the image of God in being a helper.

I hope you are encouraged as you renew your mind about what it means to be a "helper." She is certainly not "the help." It is a weighty and critical role. The woman makes up what is lacking in man. She supercharges life. She is a vital partner with man in the cause of bringing godly dominion to life at all levels. She is an immense force for good in his life—and by implication for all of humanity. The virtuous woman and excellent wife of Proverbs 31 has such an impact in her home and community. Her husband has "no lack of gain" because of her (v. 11). She makes his life fuller and richer as "she does him good, and not harm, all the days of her life" (v. 12). She is a benefit and not a hindrance. Life is a team sport, and the woman is a strategic and indispensable helper, at home and beyond.

A LIFE-GIVER

Here is an extension of this thought. The first woman was not only called a "helper fit" for Adam (Gen. 2:18), but Adam then gave her the name "Eve, because she was the mother of all living" (Gen. 3:20). Her name literally means "life-giver." This second description of Eve gives us further insight into the important purpose for which God created women. Interestingly, she was given this name before she had even given birth to her first child. The woman is a life-giver in her essence and at her core: one who bears life and one who enriches life. Therefore, in the opening chapters of Genesis, we discover that the dual purpose for which God created the woman was to be an indispensable helper to her husband and humanity as well as a life-giver.

As a sidenote, if women were designed to be life-givers, does that not underscore the evil of abortion? At the heart of a woman's character and calling is this idea that she is the mother of living things. God is saying that a woman, by definition, is to give life. It is through her that humanity will flourish. Meanwhile, the world says that a woman's right is to take life by killing her unborn child. Modern feminism is antithetical to the Bible and unnatural. It directly opposes God's character and design for women.

I want you to think through the implications of being a life-giver—not just biologically but functionally. Eve enriched Adam's life. She would give life in bearing his children, and she would bring life *to* her children. She would bring a vibrant quality of life to all of the people around her.

Remember the Proverbs 31 woman who does good to her husband for all of her days? We see vividly throughout this inspiring portrait that her husband is not the only person whose life is enriched because of her. She is a life-giver, a life-enhancer, an elixir of life and love. Her children rise up to thank God for her because she is a blessing to them (v. 28). She manages and provides for her household well (vv. 13–16, 21, 27). She is good to her maidservants (v. 15). She generously serves the poor and is attentive to the needy in her town (v. 20). Even the local merchants are benefitted by her (v. 24). She enjoys an excellent reputation in the community (vv. 30–31).

Listen to Susan Hunt, who is an author and women's Bible teacher in the Presbyterian church:

> Mothers give life, not just birth. Every woman is called to be a life-giver in every relationship and ministry God entrusts to our care. All redeemed women are mothers in Israel. Words of encouragement give life to the discouraged. Ministries of compassion infuse life into the weary and worn. Ministries of availability and hospitality beyond kith and kin model the covenant way of life. Ministries to unsaved neighbors give glimpses of life. When we live the life of *hesed* [lovingkindness], we impart life in myriad mothering roles.[2]

I want you to keep this idea at the forefront of your minds. I want you to be convinced and convicted of your purpose: "I am a life-giver. I am a daughter of Eve (Gen. 3:20). I am made in the image of God (Gen. 1:26–27). God has called me to be an indispensable helper to my husband if marriage is His will for me. But my calling is even bigger than that. I am a life-giver in all aspects: biologically, emotionally, and spiritually. These are all expressions of my created purpose. God's design for women may have been distorted by the Fall, but it is being redeemed and restored through the work of Jesus Christ and the Holy Spirit in my life."

I like the story of Christian Herter, who was governor of Massachusetts in the 1950s. He was running hard for a second term in office, and he had spent all morning and afternoon chasing votes around the county. That afternoon, just as dinner was being served at yet another political event, he was famished. As he was going down the line with his plate, he got to the place where the woman was serving the chicken. She took her tongs, put one piece of chicken on his plate, and shooed him on down the line. He stopped and said, "Excuse me, do you mind if I have another piece of chicken?" And she said, "Sorry, I can't do that. I'm supposed to give one piece of chicken to each person." He proceeded to explain the day he had just had: "I'm starving; I've been running about like crazy." But without budging she replied, "Only one per customer." A little frustrated, he turned to her and said, "Do you know who I am? I'm the governor of this state." To which she replied, "Do you know who I am? I'm the lady in charge of the chicken. Move along, mister."[3]

It's a funny and fitting story! And that is the pressing question: Do you know who you are as a woman? At the most basic level, you are an indispensable helper to man. You are God's solution to his inadequacies, and you have the potential to supercharge his life. You are also a daughter of Eve, the life-giver. There are dimensions to womanhood that men cannot rival when it comes to life-giving. You have a glorious calling, and the potential impact you can make in this world is immeasurable. Don't let anybody put you in a box.

CHAPTER 2

The Prominence
OF WOMEN IN THE BIBLE

Now that we have threaded the needle through the beginnings of Genesis, I want to continue working our way through God's Word to provide a balanced understanding of what the Bible says about women. We will see very quickly that there is a feminine thread woven throughout the tapestry of Scripture that undercuts the popular notion that the church is sexist and God is a misogynist. The heroes of the Bible, men like Abraham, Moses, David, and Paul, are well known, but the Bible is also full of heroines. These women are full of character and courage—single women, married women, and widowed women. Women of all ages, stages, and social strata feature prominently throughout the Word of God.

WOMEN IN THE OLD TESTAMENT

As the first woman created by God, Eve deserves further examination. She was an image bearer of God just as Adam was. Adam and Eve lived a pure and perfect life in the presence of God, enjoying the fruits and pleasures of Eden—that is, until they were tempted to sin by the serpent's enticements (Gen. 3:1–6). Although the woman was the one deceived by Satan and the first to fall into sin, the very first promise of the gospel comes to her and to her seed: "I will put enmity between you

[Satan] and the woman, and between your offspring and her offspring; he shall bruise your head, and you shall bruise his heel" (Gen. 3:15). This verse is considered the *protoevangelium*—the first gospel—because it is the promise that the Savior, the seed of Eve, will one day come and redeem the world by dealing the final death blow to Satan.

Did you know that the first and only character in the Bible with the honor of bestowing on God one of His names—"a God of seeing"—is actually a woman? The many names of God in Scripture are revelatory, unfolding to us His character and attributes. In Genesis 16:13, Sarah's servant Hagar "called the name of the LORD who spoke to her, 'You are a God of seeing,' for she said, 'Truly here I have seen him who looks after me.'"

Two entire books of the Old Testament are named for the extraordinary women whose stories they tell: Ruth and Esther. Ruth, a humble Moabite woman and widow in a seemingly hopeless situation, steps out in faith to follow her mother-in-law, Naomi, to a foreign land. While living a quiet life, she diligently redeems the few opportunities she has to support herself and Naomi. She endears herself to Naomi and the people of Israel through her loyalty, courage, and everyday faithfulness. God blesses her with a new homeland, a godly husband, a son, and a revered place in the lineage of the Messiah (Ruth 4:17–22).

The book of Esther is the marvelous story of how God uses one brave woman to preserve the Jews living in the Persian Empire. Through a series of events only explicable by divine providence, the beautiful, young Jewish woman Esther is handpicked by the King of Persia to be his queen at the same time that a plot to eliminate the Jews is unfolding. Her uncle Mordecai challenges her: "And who knows whether you have not come to the kingdom for such a time as this?" (Est. 4:14) She takes courage and risks her life to approach the king and make an appeal for her people, and the Lord blesses her step of faith with salvation for the Jews.

Have you noticed in the book of Proverbs that wisdom is personified as a woman? Lady Wisdom is "more precious than jewels, and nothing you desire can compare with her. Long life is in her right hand; in her left hand are riches and honor. Her ways are ways of pleasantness, and all her paths are peace. She is a tree of life to those who lay hold of her; those who hold her fast are called blessed" (Prov. 3:15–18). Everyone who desires a long, prosperous, and peaceful life needs Lady Wisdom by their side.

The Old Testament often shines a light on women acting bravely and courageously at decisive times. Miriam, Deborah, and Esther all exercised critical leadership during troubling seasons in Israel's history. Sarah, along with Abraham, persevered in faith against all odds concerning the promise of God and became the mother of many nations (Gen. 17:15–16; Rom. 4:17–21). What about the story we've heard from childhood about the Hebrew midwives in Egypt? They were ordered by Pharaoh to kill every son born of a Hebrew woman, but they chose to defy the king out of fear of God and allowed the newborn boys to live (Ex. 1:15–22). Or what about Rahab, the prostitute in the story of the conquest? She also defied the king by hiding Joshua and the spies out of the fear of the Lord (Josh. 2). Sarah and Rahab are commended and commemorated in Hebrews 11 as exemplars of faith.

That is just a sampling of the feminine thread in the 39 books of the Old Testament, yet the message is clear that God valued women and was pleased to use them in a powerful way in the unfolding of His redemptive plan.

WOMEN IN THE LIFE AND MINISTRY OF CHRIST

In the opening chapters of the New Testament, as Matthew connects Abraham and David to the coming Messiah, it is noteworthy that women—namely Rahab and Ruth—are included in the genealogy of Jesus Christ (Matt. 1:5). In the accounts of Jesus' birth, Mary and Elizabeth outshine their husbands, Joseph and Zechariah. The women are given rare insight into the gravity of the miracle that has taken place and the significance of the child in Mary's womb (Luke 1:39–56). Meanwhile, Joseph doesn't have a clue about what's going on, and Zechariah can't bring himself to believe it.

During His earthly ministry, Jesus told stories about women in the parables. What about the example of the persistent widow who goes to the unjust judge looking for justice (Luke 18:1–8)? She is a poster child for persistence in prayer. And the wonderful thing is that God is not an unjust judge—you don't have to win him over. What about the parable of the ten virgins (Matt. 25:1–13)? Five of them were rewarded for their shrewd readiness for the bridegroom's return while the other five were foolishly unprepared.

The fact that Jesus valued women was also evident in how He intentionally included them in His instruction (Luke 10:38–42). The rabbis of the day only had men as students; Jesus had female disciples. He considered it worthwhile to invest in women for the kingdom's sake, and in this He upheld creation and kingdom priorities, which are as old as time. Don't miss that little part in Luke 10 where we read about Martha scurrying about the kitchen getting some tea and scones together for Jesus. She can't believe her sister Mary is sitting in the living room and not helping her. But what does the Bible say about that?

Mary sat at Jesus' feet. That is rabbinical language. Students sat at a rabbi's feet. And in the Gospels, it is a woman who gets to sit before the greatest rabbi of them all, the teacher of all teachers. She sits at His feet and hears His word.

Women were among those whom Jesus generously healed. The woman who had been hemorrhaging blood for 12 years had spent her life's fortune on physicians who could not help her (Luke 8:43–48). Yet Jesus recognized her faith and healed her. He heals another woman with a long-term disability and lovingly calls her a "daughter of Abraham" (Luke 13:10–16). The Lord Jesus forgave women, such as the woman caught in adultery (John 8:1–11). Jesus affirmed women. He commended the poor widow who gave out of her poverty and held her up as an example (Luke 21:1–4). He visited Martha and Mary often and cared greatly for them, even weeping with them when their brother died (John 11:32–36). Jesus honors His own mother from the cross (John 19:26–27). He talks about how future generations will not forget the woman who anointed Him with perfume in worship (Matt. 26:13). The Gospel writer Luke makes it a point to mention the group of women who accompanied Jesus in His ministry and supported Him financially (Luke 8:1–3).

To women's credit, they were the last to leave the cross and the first to arrive at the empty tomb (Luke 23:50–24:12). Another observation we could make is that no woman is ever presented in the Gospels as acting against Jesus. Now, we don't want to overstate that—it is not that women aren't sinners and never do anything wrong—but it's interesting that Christ never named or denounced a woman for acting against Him. Instead, He spoke with tenderness and respect for the dignity of women, even defending them on occasions when men were pointing fingers at them (John 8:1–10).

Our Lord Jesus had a high regard for women that was not normative in His day. It ran against the grain of the prevailing culture. Here is how John MacArthur depicts the contrast:

> Women in pagan societies during biblical times were often treated with little more dignity than animals. Some of the best-known Greek philosophers—considered the brightest minds of their era—taught that women are inferior creatures by nature. Even in the Roman Empire (perhaps the very pinnacle of pre-Christian civilization) women were usually regarded as mere chattel—personal possessions of their husbands or fathers, with hardly any better standing than household slaves....
>
> Christianity, born at the intersection of East and West, elevated the status of women to an unprecedented height. Jesus' disciples included several women (Luke 8:1–3), a practice almost unheard of among the rabbis of His day.... He always treated women with the utmost dignity—even women who might otherwise be regarded as outcasts (Matt. 9:20–22; Luke 7:37–50; John 4:7–27).... Thus He exalted the position of womanhood itself.[1]

Doesn't this go to show that Christ, by whom all things were made, is consistent with the Genesis account? We see that there is a seamless flow between the Old Testament and New Testament narratives.

WOMEN IN THE EARLY CHURCH

Immediately upon Jesus' ascension to heaven, women were present alongside the apostles. Luke says, "All these [apostles] with one accord were devoting themselves to prayer, together with the women and Mary the mother of Jesus, and his brothers" (Acts 1:14). These women and others with them are presented as heroines throughout the book of Acts.

Here is a sampling of these impactful women:

1. The four daughters of Philip who prophesied (Acts 21:8–9)
2. Rhoda, the young servant girl (Acts 12:1–19)
3. Lydia, the businesswoman and church benefactress (Acts 16:11–15, 40)
4. Dorcas, a disciple "full of good works and acts of charity" (Acts 9:36–43)
5. Priscilla, Aquila's wife and co-discipler (Acts 18:2, 24–26)

How critical, valuable, distinct, and glorious is the role of the women in the early church! Women indeed build up the church. In fact, they fulfilled the important role of hosting house churches—the first church plants—and likely served those churches as well. Lydia, Priscilla, and Chloe, along with other women, are all recorded as serving the church in this capacity (Acts 16:40; Rom. 16:3–5; 1 Cor. 1:10–11). The Apostle John does not tell as much about the one he calls "the elect woman" or "the elect lady" in one of his letters, but she was likely involved in hosting a church in her home (2 John 1–2). In Romans 16, as Paul gives credit to those who have helped him in the gospel, he mentions 10 women by name. He does not hesitate to applaud and appreciate their partnership in the ministry of the gospel. He values Phoebe's service to him, telling the Romans to "welcome her in the Lord in a way worthy of the saints ... for she has been a patron of many and of myself as well" (Rom. 16:1–2). Of Euodia and Syntyche, he says, "[They] have labored side by side with me in the gospel" (Phil. 4:3).

I think you get the picture. From corner to corner, the Bible celebrates and elevates the unique and glorious contribution of women and what they have done in the life of Israel, the ministry of Jesus, and the growth of the church. As I said at the beginning, women are not the

B-team in gospel ministry or societal life. As mothers, wives, friends, businesswomen, disciples, disciple-makers, counselors, Sunday school teachers, church workers, missionaries, and more, women have served Christ as vital contributors to God's kingdom and His church.

Michael Kruger, president of Reformed Theological Seminary, gave an excellent talk in 2018 that highlighted the major role women played in the growth of the early church.[2] The record of early church history testifies to this. He says that in the second century, while the Roman Empire itself was two-thirds men and one-third women, the second-century church was comprised of two-thirds women and one-third men. In secular historical sources, Christianity was mocked as a religion of women because so many were joining the church. The writings of the early Church Fathers are sprinkled with accounts of women active in ministry. They were on the front lines of church planting and evangelism and were even martyred for the faith.

According to Kruger, women flocked to the church because they found a home there. Luke tells us of the conversions of "not a few" of the leading women in Thessalonica and the Greek women of high standing in Berea (Acts 17:4, 12). Opportunities in society were limited for women, but they could get involved and make a difference in the church. Among Christians they were treated with respect and dignity. Women and their children also found a protection within the church that they lacked in society. Christians held a high view of marriage and marital purity and condemned wicked practices of the day, such as female infanticide. The church also became a safe haven from abuse, as Scripture commands husbands to sacrificially love their wives as Christ loves the church (Eph. 5:25).

In his book *A Life Beyond Amazing*, Dr. David Jeremiah shares this story:

> Not long ago, there was a CEO of a fortune 500 company who pulled in to a service station to get gas. He went inside to pay, and when he came out he noticed his wife engaged in a deep discussion with the service station attendant. It turned out that she knew him. In fact, back in high school before she met her eventual husband, she used to date this man.
>
> The CEO got in the car, and the two drove in silence. He was feeling pretty good about himself when he finally spoke: "I bet I know what you were thinking. I bet you were thinking you're glad you married me, a Fortune 500 CEO, and not him, a service station attendant."
>
> "No, I was thinking if I'd married him, he'd be a Fortune 500 CEO and *you'd* be a service station attendant."[3]

That's the right answer! And it strikes me that this is the mistake I have made at times as a pastor. It is easy to say that women ought to thank the Lord for the church, for their husbands, and for the men in their lives. But the truth is, the church and the men of the church are equally indebted to the women in their midst. I believe we are what we are because you are what you are and you do what you do best. Women have done more to help build the church than we realize or give credit for. I'm the first to acknowledge the wonderful contribution godly women have made to my life, enriching my experience of Christ, helping me know and treasure God's Word, and building me up in my faith. I have been bolstered by the tireless support and prayers of my mother and mother-in-law, my wife, and my three daughters, who have stood by my side through decades of ministry. Other pastors' wives and women in the church have also encouraged and challenged me through their fellowship, their lives, and their words. I owe much to these saints who have faithfully fulfilled their God-given calling as women.

In their book *Lessons from the Life of Moody*, George and Donald Sweeting tell the story of how D. L. Moody took 300 young men to the house of his mother, who was confined to home due to a sprained ankle. To lift his mother's spirits, Moody asked the boys, who were standing below her window, to sing for her. Upon his command, they enthusiastically broke out in a rendition of "Jesus, Lover of My Soul." After someone prayed, Moody said to the students, "The best thing in the world for a man is to have a good mother and a good wife, and I propose three cheers for mother." The students responded with a rousing cheer for Betsy Holton Moody.[4]

As a man, son, father, and husband, I want to propose three cheers for the good and godly women in my life who have enriched, sanctified, and comforted me beyond measure—and I hope that other men will join me in that chorus.

CHAPTER 3

The Participation
OF WOMEN IN THE BIBLE

Let's look together at the broad and crucial participation of women within the community of faith. The success of the church in fulfilling Christ's mission depends on all of her members—men and women alike—doing the work of ministry (Eph. 4:11–16). This will not happen if we put women in a box and get stuck on the cannots.

Let me be clear: God has set forth certain prohibitions and parameters for women. With regard to the public gathering of the church, the apostle Paul states, "Let a woman learn quietly with all submissiveness. I do not permit a woman to teach or to exercise authority over a man; rather, she is to remain quiet" (1 Tim. 2:11–12). Scripture makes a clear case for why women cannot be pastors or elders in the church. It is also unquestionable that the Bible commands women to prioritize marriage, motherhood, and the home if they are called to such. Paul says that it lines up with sound doctrine for women to "love their husbands and children, to be self-controlled, pure, working at home, kind, and submissive to their own husbands, that the word of God may not be reviled" (Titus 2:4–5).[1]

However, with those boundaries in place, my desire is to examine and commend all that God calls women to *in addition to* being wives, mothers, and homemakers. Single and married women alike have a valuable and essential role in the building up of the body (1 Cor. 7). God wants you to know how critical your role in the church is and how you can participate in a wide range of ministries within the body of Christ. While teaching and overseeing the flock is exclusive to men called and gifted by God, that is just one function in the church (2 Tim. 2:2; Titus 1:5–9). You have a tremendous opportunity to engage in ministries that are significant and will give expression to the fullness of your spiritual gifting.

While this list is not exhaustive, let's look at the ways in which women can participate in building up Christ's church. I have drawn these applications from the New Testament as well as from aspects of the life of Israel.

THE MINISTRY OF PRAYER

God wants you to be a praying woman. Prayer is a powerful way to serve your country, your neighborhood, your church, your friends, and your family. Consider the immense impact your prayers can have—the Bible says they can move mountains and drive out demons (Matt. 17:20; Mark 9:29). James writes, "The prayer of a righteous person has great power as it is working" (James 5:16). It is a beautiful, often hidden work that can produce real results and change.

In the early church, women were actively participating in corporate prayer. They were at the first church prayer meeting in Acts 1:14, praying alongside the apostles in the upper room for the coming of the Holy Spirit. Later in the book of Acts, when Paul hears the Macedonian call for help and goes to Philippi, he finds a group of women gathered by the river to pray. It seems that there were not enough men in that community to start a synagogue, so the believers—including Lydia and these Jewish women—met down by the river to worship and pray (Acts 16:13). Anna devoted her life to the ministry of private prayer. From the time she was widowed as a young woman until the age of 84, "she did not depart from the temple, worshiping with fasting and prayer night and day" (Luke 2:36–38).

Ladies, you are an integral part of the priesthood of all believers, and prayer is a spiritual sacrifice you can offer that is pleasing to God (1 Pet. 2:5). Access to the throne of grace is an honor and a duty that you should be taking advantage of. You can storm the gates of heaven and go before the Great High Priest for your own needs and the needs of others (Heb. 4:15–16). You can do more once you have prayed, but you cannot do more *until* you have prayed.

God has uniquely gifted women with the ability to intercede with passion and compassion, and this is a gift that women ought to steward well and often. Sharon James explains it well in her book *God's Design for Women:* "The capacity to feel deeply for the needs of others with which many women are endowed can be directed towards intercession. Personal grief or joy can be focused towards prayer not only for self, but for others. In the Old Testament, Hannah's heartbreak at being infertile was transcended by her heartfelt prayers for the people of God; if she had a son he would be dedicated to God (1 Samuel 1:10–11)."[2]

Those of you who are mothers need to pray like Hannah for your children. In 1 Samuel 1:27, we find that beautiful phrase concerning Hannah and Samuel, her little boy: "For this child I prayed." Not only did God answer her prayers for a child, but He answered her prayers *for* that child—that he might be greatly used of God (1 Sam. 1:28; 2:18, 21). You should be able to look at your children and say, "For this child I prayed … and God has answered some prayers and has yet to answer others, but like the widow in the parable of the unjust judge, I am going to persevere because God is not unjust." We don't have to overcome His reluctance; we have to lay hold of His willingness.

Amelia Taylor showed such persistence as she prayed for the salvation of her son, Hudson, during his rebellious teen years. Hudson Taylor was not only saved but went on to live a life of incredible impact for God's kingdom, serving as a missionary in China for 51 years and founding the China Inland Mission. Author and pastor Tim Challies tells their story:

> She spoke to him, of course, and counseled him, but also became convinced that the best thing she could do for her son was to commit him to prayer. During a short holiday that took her away from the family home, she felt compelled to increase the length and earnestness of her prayers. One day that compulsion grew to such a degree that she determined to pray for her son until she came to a sense of assurance that God would save him. She locked herself in her room and for hours pleaded that God would extend mercy to Hudson. And then, all of a sudden, she believed that God had answered her prayer. Her heart turned from pleading to praise, and she worshipped God that he had, indeed, saved Hudson.
>
> Meanwhile, Hudson had been at home. Bored and discontent, he began looking for something to do. He wandered into his father's library and, though he pulled book after book from the shelf, found nothing of interest. Finally, he spotted a tract titled "Poor Richard." He read the story, then came to the simple words "the finished work of Christ." In that very moment, Hudson understood that Christ had done all that was necessary for salvation and the only right response was to accept that work by faith. Right there, he fell to his knees and committed his life to the Lord, promising to serve him forever. He soon learned that as he was on his knees praising God for his salvation, his mother was doing the very same thing, though many miles away.

> A few days later, he and his mother were reunited, and he immediately exclaimed, "I have some news to tell you." Before he could say anything more she replied, "I know what it is! You have given yourself to God." She explained that for days she had already been rejoicing in his salvation.[3]

I, too, am indebted to the prayers of a faithful woman: my mother. I miss her now that she is with the Lord. As I look back in my life, I have happy and holy memories of her reminding me of her prayers for me every day, as she sought God's will to be done in my life and His kingdom to come through my ministry. I truly believe that, in many ways, my life is a direct answer to my mother's prayers. That is a gift and a blessing to me. She prayed over me, my family, and my service to God for decades, and the Lord has been pleased to do a mighty work through her intercession.

THE MINISTRY OF SPIRITUAL MOTHERING

Titus 2:3–5 encapsulates the biblical call to spiritual mothering: "Older women likewise are to be reverent in behavior, not slanderers or slaves to much wine. They are to teach what is good, and so train the young women to love their husbands and children, to be self-controlled, pure, working at home, kind, and submissive to their own husbands, that the word of God may not be reviled." Younger women will grow in their faith through the means of grace available to all believers. However, in God's design, there are certain godly virtues and soft skills that they will develop best when they are taught and modeled to them by older women. Notice also that Paul tells the older woman who she ought to be before what she is to do; she should be exhibiting some measure of these virtues before teaching them to others. In Romans 16:13, Paul himself refers to an older woman who treated him like a son, saying how Rufus' mother "has been a mother to me as well."

This is life-on-life discipleship, and it ought to be taking place in your life and in the lives of those around you. The term "older women" in Scripture usually refers to women age 60 and older who have finished raising their own children in the home. But the principle applies more broadly: if you are at any level of Christian maturity, there should be another woman in your life right now that you are meeting with—whether regularly or intermittently—to build them up in godliness. As you open up your heart to her, pour into her life, strengthen her spiritually in Christ, and point her in the right direction, you are training the next generation. Pass on the pearls of wisdom you have learned from others and from your years of experience. And to the older women who are in fact well past your childrearing years: it is *not* time to kick back. Having raised your own children, God is calling you to help raise other women's children: single women, young mothers, pastors' wives, and so on. You can do that through the example of your own life and by instructing younger women in Scripture through mentoring, teaching, admonishment, and encouragement.

Dawson Trotman, the founder of Navigators, in his classic sermon entitled "Born to Reproduce," asks the important question: "Men, where is your man? Women, where is your woman? Where is the one whom you led to Christ and who is now going on with Him?"[4] Discipleship is the ministry of spiritual reproduction. Women, God has made you to be life-givers, and discipleship is a way that all women—regardless of status or life stage—can fulfill God's design as spiritual mothers.

THE MINISTRY OF GIVING

One striking thing we see in the New Testament is the patronage of the gospel through generous women. In Luke 8:1–3, we read about a group of women who followed the Lord Jesus Christ along with the disciples, and these women "provided for them out of their means" (v. 3). I think this means more than giving Jesus their packed lunch. Most commentators agree that this verse implies the women supported Jesus financially as He traveled through the cities and villages preaching the good news. They were patrons of the gospel—how beautiful is that!

I have already introduced Lydia, the wealthy businesswoman in Philippi who heard Paul's preaching, came to faith, and was baptized (Acts 16:14–15). As a new convert, Lydia enthusiastically offered up her home to the apostles, and it became a base for the church that was emerging in Philippi (Acts 16:40). Chloe and Priscilla were also successful women who used their wealth for God's kingdom and opened their homes for gospel ministry and church planting (Acts 18; 1 Cor. 1:11; 16:19).

Selina Shirley Hastings, the Countess of Huntingdon, was a modern-day Lydia who made such substantial financial contributions to the Methodist church in the 18th century that she was called "Lady Bountiful." The countess was a blue-blooded aristocrat who came to faith in Christ in the days of George Whitefield and John Wesley. She famously said she was saved by the letter M because Paul said that "not many were powerful, not many were of noble birth" who were called (1 Cor. 1:26). She was thankful for the letter M because Paul didn't say "not any" of noble birth but "not many."

Lady Huntingdon used her wealth to advance the kingdom of God. She was a major player in the establishment of the Methodist movement in England and Wales. She financed the building of more than 200 chapels and missions outposts as well as Trevecca College, a Methodist theological seminary in Wales. She was a generous philanthropist, funding missions work in colonial America and supporting the ministries of Whitefield and Wesley. She also cared for orphans.[5]

THE MINISTRY OF HOSPITALITY

Now that we have looked at the wealthy women who volunteered their homes for church plants, it is only natural that we highlight service through hospitality. This is a natural gift and ministry for all women who have and keep their own homes (Titus 2:5). Maintaining a warm, orderly, and welcoming home is a mark of biblical femininity. Women bear this responsibility first as a benefit to their husbands and children and then as a blessing to the church and the community. A widow is given a special ministry privilege if she has a reputation for good works, including showing hospitality (1 Tim. 5:9–10).

The Bible commands all believers to practice hospitality (Rom. 12:13). The Greek word for hospitality—*philoxenia*—means "love for strangers." The author of Hebrews writes, "Let brotherly love continue. Do not neglect to show hospitality to strangers, for thereby some have entertained angels unawares" (Heb. 13:1–2). There is always a risk to opening up your home to strangers, but the reward could be great—you could be serving an angel or making a gospel impact on someone. So I want to ask you this: Are you being selfish with the home God has given you? Do you see your home as a stewardship to use for His glory? Do you have people over to show them brotherly love or gospel compassion?

The priority of hospitality is providing a place of warmth and welcome to strangers—not impressing them. Sharon James says it well: "Hospitality involves making others truly feel they are welcomed, at home with us. It is different to 'entertaining', with all the connotations of going all out to impress or repaying social obligations. Over-elaborate preparations may have a negative effect on guests, as well as on the exhausted hostess."[6] So, I am not talking about being house-proud. You don't need fancy silverware or Royal Doulton china to extend hospitality. It is not a money issue. It is an attitude issue. As long as your home is clean and orderly and you have a heart for people, extend the gift of hospitality! It is a *gospel* issue. It is a matter of love for friends, family, and the unsaved around you. And given the fact that it is increasingly more difficult to get our neighbors to church, I think our homes will once again become the front line of gospel impact as it was in the early church.

In *The Gospel Comes with a House Key*, Rosaria Butterfield shares her own testimony of faith and the power of hospitality. Read this book if you get a chance. Rosaria was a lesbian feminist and a tenured professor at Syracuse University. She was a strong and vocal advocate of the LGBTQ cause. She was befriended by a Christian couple who invited her to their home and welcomed her at their dining table. Slowly but surely, over many visits and conversations together, Rosaria's guard came down, her heart softened, and her life was changed through faith in Jesus Christ. Today, Rosaria is a pastor's wife, a speaker, and an author of several books. Now, she lends her voice to advocate the cause of Christ—thanks in part to the loving and persistent hospitality of one couple.

THE MINISTRY OF MERCY AND COMFORT

In the book of Isaiah, God likens Himself to a gentle mother—one who shows tender compassion and comforts others (Isa. 49:15; 66:13). Women reflect the image of God in these ways and can utilize these strengths to aid hurting and needy people through mercy ministry.

During His time on earth, even our Lord was cared for and enriched through the kind service of godly women: "When he was in Galilee, they followed him and ministered to him, and there were also many other women who came up with him to Jerusalem" (Mark 15:41). These women loved Jesus and were eager to stay by His side and meet His practical needs. Jesus teaches that we can even minister to Him today by ministering to the needy around us—feeding the hungry, welcoming strangers, clothing the naked, visiting the sick, and reaching out to those in prison (Matt. 25: 31–40). How amazing is it that when we do acts of charity, we are, in a sense, ministering directly to our Lord? One such woman in the early church who "was full of good works and acts of charity" was Dorcas (Acts 9:36–43). She seems to have touched many lives because when she died, she was surrounded by grieving widows who showed Peter the clothing and tunics she had made for them. Peter miraculously brought Dorcas back to life, and many rejoiced and put their faith in Christ. The godly widows Paul speaks of in 1 Timothy 5 were also known for caring for the afflicted (v. 10). In short, women were actively involved in mercy ministries—in comforting the grieving, in clothing the poor, in healing the hurt.

Many women, along with the church in that day, devoted themselves to the "pure religion" of fostering and adopting orphans (James 1:27). This was so prevalent in the early church that Roman critics of Christianity admitted in conversations with Christian apologists that Christians looked after Roman citizens better than Rome itself. The ancient Romans had an atrocious practice of abandoning their infants because of poverty, birth defects, unknown paternity, or any other reason. They called this practice "exposure" because the babies were left exposed to the elements.[7] The Christians at that time would go through the streets and rescue these precious babies.

Do you see those in need around you, both in the church and outside, and give your time and energy to serve them? You can serve fellow believers by delivering a meal to the sick and suffering, shopping for groceries for the elderly, visiting and praying with those who are sick, babysitting for a struggling mother, and so much more. There are myriad ways to minister to the needy in the world: fostering and adopting children, going on a short-term mission trip, volunteering at a food bank or a crisis pregnancy center, buying a meal for a homeless person in your town, stuffing envelopes for the charity that your church partners with—all while sharing the gospel of Jesus with your words and good deeds. Even small acts of service can have a lasting impact for the kingdom of God.

THE MINISTRY OF THE WORD

Women are not exempt from the command of Colossians 3:16, which is for all believers: "Let the word of Christ dwell in you richly, teaching and admonishing one another in all wisdom, singing psalms and hymns and spiritual songs, with thankfulness in your hearts to God." You as women must soak deeply in the truths of Scripture and use it to instruct and build up others in the faith. Although you will not be teaching men in church gatherings, you will have many relationships and settings in which you can—and must—be a teacher of God's Word.

You are to teach your children.

Was it not said of Timothy that he knew the Scriptures from childhood (2 Tim. 3:14–15)? Timothy's sincere faith was the legacy of his grandmother, Lois, and his mother, Eunice, who faithfully taught him sound doctrine and modeled it by their lives (2 Tim. 1:5). Solomon also grew in wisdom and knowledge because of his mother's instruction (Proverbs 1:8; 31:1).

Mothers, you can be the single greatest influence for Christ in your child's life. Whether you have little ones or teenagers, your days will be filled with everyday moments to teach them God's truth "as you go." Moses stressed the importance of this responsibility to pass on God's commands to the next generation: "And the words that I command you today shall be on your heart. You shall teach them diligently to your children, and shall talk of them when you sit in your house, and when you walk by the way, and when you lie down, and when you rise" (Deut. 6:6–7). This is your duty.

Even if you don't have children of your own, you can come alongside families and help sow God's truth into their children's hearts. Spend time with your friends' children and talk to them about who God is. Teach a Sunday school class. Volunteer for your church's Vacation Bible School. You can be an instrument in bringing these little ones to Christ.

You are to teach other women.

We have already looked at the command in Titus 2 for older women to teach younger women. This can be done informally or formally through discipleship and mentoring relationships. There are many young women who are hungry for God's Word and for someone to speak truth into their lives as they are trying to figure out life themselves! Make yourself available for discipleship in the church. Meet one-on-one with a younger woman or form a small group and study a book of the Bible together. Memorize verses together. Do a topical Bible study on a common area of struggle, such as anxiety or discipline.

With training in the Scriptures, you can also teach women through the ministry of counseling. This is a targeted form of discipleship in which you help and guide women who are dealing with more severe and urgent issues, such as addictions, marital infidelity, or mental health problems. Oftentimes, women struggling with these issues turn to the pastor for counseling when they could benefit from being instructed by another woman who understands their unique frame and can relate personally with what they are facing. If you have a strong knowledge of the Word and its application, there are many avenues to receive specific training in biblical counseling.

You can instruct others alongside your husband in private discipleship.

Remember the story of Apollos in Acts 18? He was an able and powerful teacher of God's Word, but he had some blind spots. There were some gaps in his theological understanding. Priscilla and her husband, Aquila, took him aside privately and "explained to him the way of God more accurately" (Acts 18:26). A woman was involved in helping a man who knew the Scriptures know them even better! And Apollos in turn was able to help others in their faith more effectively.

You can teach through writing books.

Women can wield enormous influence for the Lord through the writing of Christian books geared toward training a wider audience of women. There are many excellent and theologically robust books by women authors, many of which I have referenced for this book. These women and others—such as Nancy Guthrie, Ruth Chou Simons, and Nancy DeMoss Wolgemuth—have delved deeply into the biblical role of women, and I am indebted to them for their insights and perspectives.

As God calls you to be instructors of the Word in certain spheres—from your homes to your friendships to the church—it is of paramount importance that you are theologically sound. You need to know how to study your Bible and how to teach Scripture accurately. Be a Berean—a faithful and discerning student of the Word. Take advantage of any equipping in the Word that your church makes available to you. This exhortation was for Timothy as a young pastor, but it applies to anyone in a position to teach God's holy Word: "Do your best to present yourself to God as one approved, a worker who has no need to be ashamed, rightly handling the word of truth" (2 Tim. 2:15).

THE MINISTRY OF SONG AND WORSHIP

In 1 Corinthians 11, as Paul corrects some practices at the church in Corinth, he makes it clear that although women weren't leading or teaching in the worship service, they were participating through prayer and prophecy—the public proclamation of truth.

Miriam, the sister of Aaron, led the women in worship (Ex. 15:20–21). And what about the mother of our Lord Jesus Christ, Mary, and her Magnificat in Luke 1:46? Women wrote hymns, sang in worship, and played instruments. Women led other women in worship. Women joined with men in the congregation of the believing community to sing God's praise. If you have an ability and gift for music, join the church choir or worship team and bless the church with your gifts. We need women to sing—to make a joyful noise unto the Lord! We need the female nightingales in the congregation to balance out the gales in the night.

The hymn writer Fanny Crosby had a deep devotion to the Lord born out of tragedy. It was out of this devotion that she wrote thousands of moving and doctrinally rich hymns, many of which we sing in the church today. Fanny became blind when she was just a few months old because a quack doctor misapplied some medicine. As she dealt with blindness her whole life, she said that her blindness helped her see God and put her in touch with the spiritual. Her life was a heartache. She lived with blindness, she was fatherless, and she grew up in poverty. Her mother's second marriage led her into a cult and almost drove Fanny to despair. Fanny's own marriage was a challenge, and for a period of time, she lived separated from her husband. She went through sorrow upon sorrow, but in the middle of it all, she saw God. In the middle of it all, God led her to write the soul-stirring hymns we sing in our worship services, such as "Blessed Assurance" and "Jesus, Keep Me Near the Cross."

One writer had this insight about Franny Crosby: "Preachers, theologians and Bible scholars who would not permit a woman to speak or teach in a worship service week after week sang her hymns and profited from her ministry."[8] The church greatly profits from women who sing and write songs of worship or play their instruments excellently unto the Lord (Ps. 150; Col. 3:16–17). My church benefits every Sunday from a wonderful group of women who help us worship.

Fanny Crosby was buried at a ripe old age. When her family buried her, they put a simple headstone above her remains that simply read: "Aunt-Fanny: She hath done what she could." That's a great statement, and it's a verse out of the Gospels about a certain devout woman: "She has done what she could" (Mark 14:8).

Ladies, do what you can for Christ, through Christ (Phil. 4:13). What God allows you to do is broad, bold, and beautiful. Don't be boxed in because of unbiblical thinking, because of the bad advice you have been given by others, or because of an overreach by even good churches. God has called you to be indispensable helpers and life-givers. I pray that you will think through this wide-ranging menu of ministries that are open to you and get busy serving in your local body of believers (Rom. 12:1). Join the endless line of women parading across the Bible and redemptive history who enhanced the life of the church, won people to Christ, proclaimed Jesus' name, blessed the saints, and supported the spread of the gospel. Now you go, girl!

Acknowledgements

I am indebted to God for the gift of the women in my life who have made me what I am and allowed me to be who I am. I want to thank my dear mother, who was a faithful cheerleader and intercessor for me until the day she went home to be with the Lord. Thank you to June's mother, May—a mother-in-law who has been a good friend and kindhearted soul to her son-in-law. Thank you to my beloved wife, June, and my daughters, Angela, Laura, and Beth, for their love and support day in and day out. And thank you to the many women in our church and other churches who have blessed us across the years, enriching our home and me.

I also want to express my appreciation to all those who have helped bring this little book to life. Many thanks to Dean Samsvick, Jerry Motto, Danielle Bracey, and the excellent team at Know The Truth—your tireless effort behind the scenes allows the truth of God to reach so many. I want to give special thanks to Joan Shim for her assistance in the penning of this book as well as Briana Sukert for her editing input. Finally, thank you to Kindred Community Church and her leaders—I am strengthened by your loving support, commitment, and partnership in the gospel.

ENDNOTES

INTRODUCTION

[1] Michael Reeves, *The Unquenchable Flame* (Nashville: B&H Publishing Group, 2010), 128.

[2] Tony Merida, "Tony Merida on the Vital Importance of Women in the Church's Mission." Posted March 29, 2019. *The Gospel Coalition: https://www.thegospelcoalition.org/video/tony-merida-vital-importance-women-churchs-mission/* (August 19, 2021).

[3] Michelle DeRusha, *50 Women Every Christian Should Know: Learning from Heroines of the Faith* (Ada, MI: Baker Books, 2014), 117.

[4] Source unknown

[5] Michelle DeRusha, *Katharina and Martin Luther* (Ada, MI: Baker Books, 2017), 197.

CHAPTER 1:
THE PURPOSE OF WOMEN IN THE BIBLE

[1] John MacArthur, *The MacArthur Study Bible, English Standard Version* (Wheaton: Crossway, 2010), 20.

[2] Susan Hunt and Barbara Thompson, *The Legacy of Biblical Womanhood* (Wheaton, IL: Crossway, 2003), 169.

[3] Bits & Pieces, "Chicken Lady." May 28, 1992, 5–6. *Bible.org: https://bible.org/illustration/chicken-lady* (August 18, 2021).

CHAPTER 2:
THE PROMINENCE OF WOMEN IN THE BIBLE

1. John MacArthur, "The Biblical Portrait of Women: Setting the Record Straight." *Grace to You: https://www.gty.org/library/articles/a265* (October 23, 2021).

2. Michael Kruger, "The Dynamic Ministry of Women in Early Christianity." Posted September 29, 2018. *The Gospel Coalition: https://www.thegospelcoalition.org/podcasts/tgc-podcast/dynamic-ministry-women-early-christianity/* (August 18, 2021).

3. Dr. David Jeremiah, *A Life Beyond Amazing* (Nashville: Thomas Nelson, 2017), 160.

4. George Sweeting and Donald Sweeting, *Lessons from the Life of Moody* (Chicago: Moody Press, 1989), 27–28.

CHAPTER 3:
THE PARTICIPATION OF WOMEN IN THE BIBLE

1. For further study on the biblical guidelines for women in the church, I recommend *Different by Design: Discovering God's Will for Today's Man and Woman* by John MacArthur, *The Grand Design: Male and Female He Made Them* by Owen Strachan and Gavin Peacock, and *Men and Women in the Church* by Kevin DeYoung.

2. Sharon James, *God's Design for Women* (Darlington: Evangelical Press, 2002), 119.

3. Tim Challies, "The Power of a Praying Mother (Christian Men and Their Godly Moms)." Posted April 1, 2017. *Challies.com: https://www.challies.com/articles/the-power-of-a-praying-mother/* (August 18, 2021).

4. Dawson Trotman, Born to Reproduce, 1955. *New Orleans Baptist Theological Seminary: https://www.nobts.edu/discipleship/downloadable-documents1/spiritual-formation-folder/Born%20to%20reproduce%20Dawson%20Trotman.pdf* (August 18, 2021).

5   BibleMesh, "I Thank God for the Letter 'M'". Posted November 26, 2020. *BibleMesh: https://biblemesh.com/blog/i-thank-god-for-the-letter-m/* (August 18, 2021).

6   James, *God's Design for Women*, 136.

7   N.S. Gill, "Roman Family and the Exposure of Infants." Updated February 2, 2019. *ThoughtCo: https://www.thoughtco.com/roman-exposure-of-infants-118370* (September 8, 2021).

8   Ray Beeson, *The Hidden Price of Greatness* (Wheaton, IL: Tyndale, 1991), 94.